REALLY BIG Questions FOR DARING THINKERS

KINGFISHER
LONDON & NEW YORK

Copyright © 2009, 2024 by Macmillan Publishers International Ltd
Text copyright © 2009, 2024 by Stephen Law
Illustrations copyright © 2009, 2024 by Nishant Choksi
www.nishantchoksi.com

First published in 2022
This edition published in 2024 in the United States by Kingfisher,
120 Broadway, New York, NY 10271
Kingfisher is an imprint of Macmillan Children's Books, London.
All rights reserved.

First published as *Really Really Big Questions* in 2009

Distributed in the U.S. and Canada by Macmillan,
120 Broadway, New York, NY 10271

EU representative: Macmillan Publishers Ireland Ltd, 1st Floor,
The Liffey Trust Centre, 117-126 Sheriff Street Upper, Dublin 1, D01 YC43

Library of Congress Cataloging-in-Publication data has been applied for.

ISBN: 978-0-7534-7829-5 (HC)
978-0-7534-7994-0 (PB)

Kingfisher books are available for special promotions and premiums.
For details contact: Special Markets Department, Macmillan,
120 Broadway, New York, NY 10271.

For more information, please visit www.kingfisherbooks.com

Printed in China
1 3 5 7 9 8 6 4 2
1TR/0324/UG/WKT/140WF

Note to readers: The website addresses listed in this book are correct at the time
of going to print. However, due to the ever-changing nature of the Internet, website addresses and
content can change. Websites can contain links that are unsuitable
for children. The publisher cannot be held responsible for changes in website
addresses or content, or for information obtained through a third party.
We strongly advise that Internet searches are supervised by an adult.

MIX
Paper | Supporting
responsible forestry
FSC® C116313

REALLY **BIG** Questions FOR **DARING** THINKERS

Dr. Stephen Law

Illustrated by
Nishant Choksi

CONTENTS

CHAPTER 3
The Good, the Bad, and the Ugly

CHAPTER 4
Seeing and Believing

THE BIGGEST
AND STRANGEST
QUESTIONS OF ALL

DR. STEPHEN LAW

This is a book of questions—it includes some of the biggest and weirdest questions ever asked.

Have you ever wondered, "Where did everything come from?" "Are some people psychic?" "Is time travel possible?" or "What makes stealing wrong?" You will find all these questions in this book.

While I'm pretty sure I know the answer to many of these questions, there are lots of others I am not sure about. In fact, some are questions that the world's greatest thinkers are still struggling with today!

Some are *scientific* questions—questions like:

Can you bend a spoon with your mind?
What is stuff made of?
Does astrology really work?

How do scientists try to answer these questions? By *observing* and *performing experiments*.

If Molly says she can bend a spoon with her mind, scientists can test Molly's claim by doing an experiment. They can put Molly in a science lab, place a spoon out of her reach, make sure that there's no way Molly can bend the spoon by cheating, and put sensors on the spoon to see if it really does bend.

Other questions in this book are *philosophical* questions. They include questions like these:

Did someone design the universe?
What is the meaning of life?
Is it wrong to design a baby?

One interesting fact about many of these questions is that they seem to be *questions that science cannot answer*. Some people think that science can answer every question. But that's not true.

Take questions about right and wrong. Scientists learn many things by observing and performing scientific experiments. Scientists also make new things possible—they can allow us to make even bigger bombs, for example. But while scientists can do these things, science can't tell us whether these are things we *should* do. When it comes to right and wrong, science leaves us largely in the dark. If we want to know the answer, we have to figure it out in some other way. That's what philosophers try to do.

Feel free to jump into this book wherever you like. And remember: *think for yourself!* Even when I think I know the answer, you should still make up your *own* mind. After all, I've been known to make mistakes!

1

THE GREAT BIG UNIVERSE PUZZLE

We inhabit a vast universe. Our planet, Earth, revolves around the Sun, which is just one of the many billions of stars that make up our galaxy, the Milky Way. And there are many billions of such galaxies.

Where did all this come from? Why is it here? Was it designed by God? And how did living things appear?

These are some of the big questions we try to answer in this chapter.

WHERE DID EVERYTHING COME FROM?

Have you ever looked up on a starlit night and wondered—*where did all this come from?* Why does the universe exist? Why is there *something*, rather than nothing?

Scientists say that the universe started with an enormous explosion —called the big bang—in which all matter and energy, and even time and space, began.

This happened about 13 billion years ago. In other words, thirteen thousand groups of one million years ago—a very, very long time ago.

"If you want to make an apple pie from scratch, you must first create the universe."

Carl Sagan (1934–1996)
American astronomer

WHAT HAPPENED BEFORE THE BIG BANG?

If time itself began with the big bang, then there was no *before* the big bang. That's a very weird thought, isn't it?

Usually when something happens, we can talk about before and after. Take an explosion at a factory, for example. We might say that before the explosion, there was a big fuel leak. That was what caused the explosion. And then, after the explosion, the fire department arrived to put out the fire.

But the big bang is different. It has an after, of course. *But there is no before.* The big bang marks the beginning of time itself.

So, it seems that nothing happened before the big bang because there was no time for it to happen in.

WHERE DID THE BIG BANG COME FROM?

So, what *caused* the big bang? Where did it come from? If there was no space and no time before the big bang, then it must have come from *nothing*.

But how did *nothing* produce the big bang, the universe, planets, chocolate, dinosaurs, iPads, *everything*? How can all that come from nothing? *How can nothing produce something?*

WHAT IS NOTHING?

So there was no time or space or matter or energy or anything at all. *Pop*—the universe appears! From nothing! But *how*? How could the universe come from absolutely nothing at all?

It's certainly a very strange and unusual sort of nothing that we're talking about, isn't it?

Usually, when we talk about there being nothing, we mean there exists, say, *an empty bit of space.* When I say, "There's nothing in my cup," I mean that, right now, the space inside my cup is empty. There's no tea or juice or water in there.

And when I say, "I'm doing nothing right now," I mean that at this moment in time, I'm not doing anything in particular.

But when we ask, "Why is there something rather than nothing?" we are talking about a much weirder sort of nothing.

The sort of nothing we are talking about is this: not only is there no stuff, and nothing going on, there's no time or space in which anything could exist or in which anything could go on.

We're talking about *absolute* nothing.

CAN I THINK ABOUT NOTHING?

Try thinking about absolute nothing. Can you do it?

Remember, you mustn't be thinking about a black and empty space. For if you're thinking about a black and empty space, you are still thinking about something—that black and empty space. You are supposed to be thinking about *absolute nothing*.

I am not sure I can think about absolute nothing. I just seem to end up not thinking about anything.

But maybe *you* can do it?

HOW CAN SOMETHING COME FROM NOTHING?

Perhaps there is something wrong with this question. If we cannot even think about absolute nothing, maybe that's because it doesn't make sense. But then neither does this question.

Nothing
by N. O. Body

DID SOMEONE DESIGN THE UNIVERSE?

Suppose that, while walking along a beach, you come across a watch lying in the sand. You see that the watch has a *purpose*. There is something it is for—to tell the time. And you see that it has been carefully constructed to fulfill that purpose.

Isn't it reasonable to suppose the watch has a designer? Surely it is. It's far more likely that it was designed by some intelligent being than that the various bits and pieces should have been formed and put together by chance.

Can't we draw a similar conclusion about, say, the eye? It too has a purpose—to allow the creature attached to it to see. And the eye is extremely well suited to that purpose.

An eye is made up of lots of different parts, all of which have to fit together perfectly before it can do its job. So, some people believe that the eye must have a designer, too. They believe it was also designed by an intelligent being.

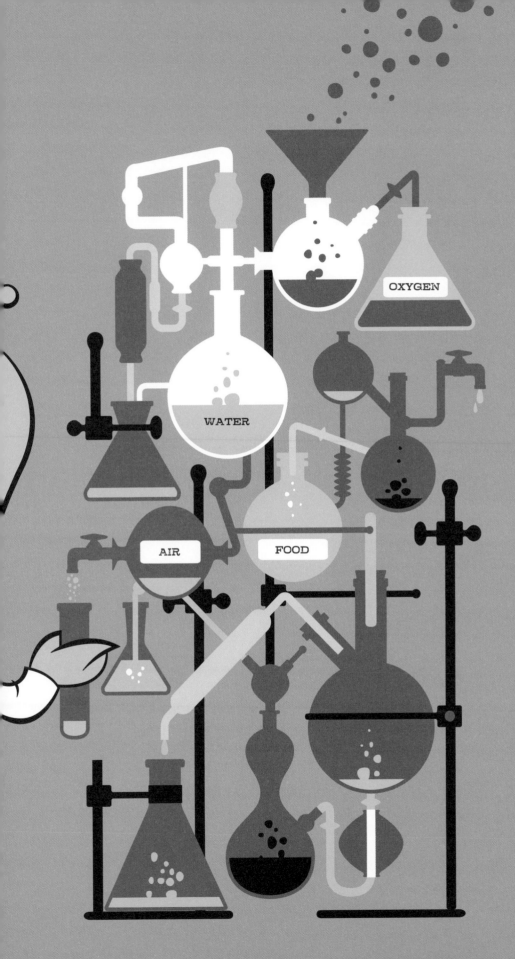

Some people believe that not only do eyes, and living things generally, have a designer, but so too does the whole universe and everything it contains. They think that planet Earth was carefully designed for us to inhabit—there's just the right kind of food, just the right amount of water, and there is oxygen in the air.

How likely is it that the world should fit us so perfectly, just by chance? Surely, some say, there must be a designer who designed the world for us!

But if a designer designed the universe, who designed the designer?

The writer Douglas Adams once told this little story about a puddle:

Imagine a puddle waking up one morning and thinking, "This is an interesting world I find myself in, an interesting hole I find myself in. Fits me rather neatly, doesn't it? In fact, it fits me staggeringly well—must have been made to have me in it!"

The puddle makes a mistake—he thinks that because his hole fits him so well, it must have been designed for him. But of course, it wasn't. Adams suspects that this is a mistake some of us make, too, when we think, *"Look at how this world fits us so neatly. It must have been designed for us!"*

If the hole wasn't designed to fit the puddle, why suppose Earth was designed to fit us?

WHERE DO LIVING THINGS COME FROM?

In our forests, jungles, deserts, and oceans, there is an extraordinary range of living things—from enormous blue whales to tiny jewellike insects. *But where did all these different species come from?*

Through the ages, people have told different stories to explain how living things appeared.

The Pelasgians, who lived long ago in Greece, told a story about Eurynome. She danced across the water to make a wind, which she rolled into a snake. The snake, Ophion, made Eurynome pregnant with an enormous egg. He squeezed and squeezed the egg until Earth and all its animals and plants spilled out.

Or take the Bible. It says the world was made by God in six days. On the third day, God made all the plants; on the fifth, creatures of the sea and sky; and on the sixth day, he made the land creatures.

These stories from different times, places, and religions are certainly strange and wonderful. But are any of them *true*?

WHAT IS EVOLUTION?

Today, almost all scientists agree about how life appeared on Earth. They say the different species emerged very slowly, over many millions of years, by a process called *evolution*.

At first, there were only simple life forms on our planet. As these simple things reproduced, they sometimes changed slightly. Gradually, over enormous periods of time, these small changes added up to bigger changes, until new, more complex kinds of creatures began to emerge.

But why would new species change in this way?

Charles Darwin discovered the process of *natural selection*, which provides one explanation for why species evolve. When living things reproduce, their offspring may be slightly different. Changes suited to a particular habitat are more likely to be passed on to the next generation than those that are not. So, living things gradually adapt to fit their surroundings.

Take the polar bear and brown bear—they are very closely related, but the polar bear has evolved to suit a cold climate. It has thick fur, large feet for walking on snow, and a white coat for camouflage. The brown bear has no such adaptations and would not survive long in the Arctic.

Brrrrrrr

DID WE ALL REALLY USED TO BE MONKEYS?

Sometimes people say, "Scientists claim we used to be monkeys!" But that's not quite right. Scientists say we share a *common ancestor* with today's apes.

Just as you and your cousin have grandparents in common, so you and those monkeys you see at the zoo have a common ancestor. But that common ancestor lived *millions of years ago!*

Monkeys, apes, and humans are all primates. And all three share certain common characteristics—like ten fingers and ten toes, flattish faces, and large brains. But there are obvious differences, too—and those differences are due to evolution.

Scientists say that our closest living relatives are chimpanzees, but that doesn't mean that we used to *be* chimpanzees. We have been evolving separately for about the past six million years. From a common primate ancestor, two unique species have developed—chimpanzees and *Homo sapiens sapiens* (that's us).

WHAT IS STUFF MADE OF?

A very long time ago—about two and a half thousand years ago—philosophers in ancient Greece wondered about the world. And they wondered about what everything was made of.

One philosopher, called Anaximenes, thought that everything was *air*. Things like earth and water don't seem to be air, do they? Still, Anaximenes thought that earth and water are what you get if you squash air up. Squash air up enough and it turns into water. Squash it up some more and you get earth.

Anaximenes

Thales

Heraclitus

Before Anaximenes, another philosopher, Thales, supposed that everything was *water*.

And after Anaximenes, there came Heraclitus, who thought that, deep down, the world was *fire*.

Eventually, a philosopher named Empedocles decided that none of these theories was quite right. He said the world was made up of not one but *four* elements—earth, air, fire, and water.

The theory that the world is made up of these four elements became popular and lasted for a long time—more than two thousand years.

Empedocles

WHAT ARE ATOMS?

In about 420 B.C., the philosopher Democritus invented the word *atom*, which comes from the Greek word *atomos*, meaning "uncuttable." He thought that ordinary physical objects can be cut up into parts, and that those parts can be chopped up into smaller parts, but that eventually there will be parts that cannot be chopped up any more. These uncuttable parts are the "atoms" out of which everything is made, thought Democritus.

Democritus

Today, what scientists call atoms have parts—electrons, protons, and neutrons—and even these parts have parts!

IS EVERYTHING PHYSICAL?

The idea that everything can be boiled down to just one thing is still popular. Many people believe that everything is physical and has qualities such as size and shape.

Clearly lots of things are physical objects. The Eiffel Tower, pudding, planets, and ants are all physical objects. But what about *love*? And *thoughts*? Are they physical? You can't pick up love or bang your head against it. And you can't catch thoughts in a net. But then you can't catch a *rainbow* in a net either—yet a rainbow is part of the physical world.

WHAT IS THE MEANING OF LIFE?

Does life have a meaning? Are we here for a purpose?

Some people believe there is a reason we are here—we were designed by God to love and obey Him.

Others believe that while some things are made for a purpose—a hammer is made to bang in nails, and an egg timer is made to time boiling eggs—we're not. Yes, we're here, but we are not here for anything in particular, not in the way hammers and egg timers are. It's up to us to decide what we're here for. We can choose our own purpose and meaning.

If we do have a purpose, would that make our lives *meaningful*?

Suppose we were designed for a purpose. Suppose aliens have been breeding humans on Earth for a reason—to wash their smelly underpants! They are coming soon to pick us all up in flying saucers and take us to their planet where we will work day and night scrubbing the stains from their alien underwear.

When we start cleaning their underpants, we discover we love doing it. We love doing it because we are designed to find the smell lovely. We never want to do anything else. We finally feel happy in a way we've never felt before!

Would the fact that we are designed for a purpose—to wash alien underpants—really make our lives meaningful?

Not really. Yes, we would be happy and *fulfilling our purpose*, but that wouldn't mean our lives were meaningful, would it?

It seems that fulfilling a purpose and having a meaningful existence aren't always the same thing.

2

MYSTERIOUS MINDS AND ROBOTS THAT THINK

In a way, my mind seems to be the thing I know best. Yes, there are lots of things I might be wrong about. I might be mistaken in thinking I am awake—perhaps I'm really asleep in bed, dreaming. But surely, I can't be wrong in thinking that I have a mind? Just by thinking that thought, I prove I have one!

So I think I can be absolutely certain that I have a mind. But what is my mind? The more I think about this question, the more puzzled I become . . .

WHAT IS IT LIKE

We can do many things that a cabbage can't—like *think* and feel *emotions*. That's because, unlike a cabbage, we have *minds*. A dog also has a mind. He can feel pain and remember things. But do *all* animals have minds? What about *slugs* or *flies*? It's difficult to say!

Bats do seem to have minds. They seem to experience the world around them. But what is a bat's mind *like*, do you think?

The smaller bats "see" using sound. They send out squeaking noises and, with their big ears, listen to the echoes bouncing back off insects and cave walls. That's how they hunt in the dark.

While we know bats can do these things, we don't know what it's like for the bat when it experiences the world in this way. What is it like to be a bat *from the inside*?

No matter how much we know about what's going on physically inside a bat when it "sees" using sound, we will never know what the experience itself is like— not even if we cut the bat open and prod around inside its body. Its mind will *still* be hidden.

So it seems that the minds of other creatures— and even other people—are hidden in a rather peculiar way. Minds are a bit of a mystery!

TO BE A BAT?

WHAT DOES MY BRAIN DO?

Inside your skull there's a sludgy, gray organ called your brain. It looks like a big walnut. Your brain is made of billions of cells called neurons, which are woven together in a very complicated way, like a net.

So what does your brain *do*? Well, it seems to be a sort of central control room. It *sends out electrical signals* to the rest of your body. When you wriggle your legs, for example, they move because neurons in your brain "fire," sending signals to your leg muscles.

Your brain also *receives* electrical signals from your body. When you see, light enters your eye and makes a little image on the retina at the back of the eye. The retina is covered in tiny light-sensitive cells that transmit electrical signals to your brain. That's what allows you to see. Your brain also receives signals from your ears (allowing you to hear) and tongue (allowing you to taste), and so on.

Your brain interacts with your *mind*. What happens in one can affect what happens in the other.

What happens in your brain can certainly affect what happens in your mind. Right now, you are *experiencing* this book—seeing it, thinking about it, perhaps liking or disliking it—because light entering your eye is making things happen in your brain.

And what happens in your mind can affect what happens in your body. If your mind decides to move your legs, it is your brain that sends out the electrical signals that make them move around.

IS MY MIND MY BRAIN?

So your mind and your body interact. But could your mind actually *be* your brain?

Suppose you have an experience—you taste a very sweet orange, for example. Could that experience *just be* something happening in your brain? Could it *just be* some of your neurons firing?

Your experience of that tangy taste doesn't seem like neurons firing in your brain, does it? But that doesn't mean it's not something going on in your brain. After all, things aren't always what they seem. Earth doesn't seem like a great ball hurtling around the Sun at enormous speed, yet that's just what it is.

So while your experiences might not *seem* like things happening in your brain, maybe that's what they *are. Maybe your mind is the same thing as your brain.*

Philosophers and scientists disagree about that! What do *you* think?

BRAIN BURN!

I can *imagine* myself floating around without legs, arms, or a brain. Does this show that I *really could* exist without a body?

COULD A ROBOT

Imagine that one day scientists build an amazing robot. Inside its head is a robot brain made out of wires and computer chips. This robot brain is designed to do the same job as a human brain. It receives electrical signals from the robot body's robot ears, eyes, nose, tongue, and skin. And it sends out electrical signals to make the robot body walk, talk, and move around. So the robot *behaves just like a normal human being.* Only it's not made out of flesh, blood, and bone. It's made out of *metal and plastic.*

Suppose you say, "Hello, what's your name?" to this robot. Just like normal human ears, its robot ears will pick up the sound of your voice and send electrical signals to its robot brain. Its robot brain will then respond just like your human brain, sending out electrical signals to its mouth. So it will talk back to you just like a normal human. *The robot will seem to be able to think.*

In fact, if we were to put this robot inside plastic human-looking skin, so that it looked exactly like a human being, no one would be able to tell it *wasn't* human.

True, this robot wouldn't have blood pumping through its veins, or a heart and lungs. It wouldn't need to eat or drink. It would be a plastic and metal *machine.*

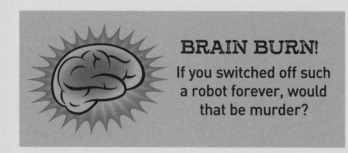

BRAIN BURN!
If you switched off such a robot forever, would that be murder?

THINK?

So, although the robot *looks* like a human, it isn't one. Does that mean that although it also *appears to think* like a human, it can't *really* think?

Some would say yes. The robot *behaves* as if it has a mind. But there are no real thoughts and feelings going on. The robot is just a machine— a machine that creates the *illusion* that it thinks and feels.

Others disagree. They think it doesn't matter what sort of *stuff* you are made of. What matters is what you can *do*. This robot behaves just like us. So if we have minds, it must have a mind, too.

If you think this robot doesn't have a mind, what do you think we would need to add to it in order for it to have real thoughts and experiences? How would the robot need to change in order for it to be *really* thinking?

CAN YOU BEND A SPOON WITH YOUR MIND?

I doubt it, but give it a try. Nobody has ever proved in a science lab that they can bend a spoon with their mind. I have seen people *appear* to bend spoons that way. But most have admitted that they were just performing a magic trick.

Here's one of the simplest and easiest spoon-bending tricks: hold a spoon at its neck, just beneath the bowl part. Now waggle the spoon back and forth. The spoon appears to bend, doesn't it?

ARE SOME PEOPLE PSYCHIC?

Many people say they are psychic. Some claim to be *mediums* who communicate with the dead. Some insist they have a miraculous ability to see into the future. A few psychics even appear on TV or write for newspapers. Some make money running *psychic hotlines*—you make an often expensive phone call to the psychic, and they might then tell you about your dead relatives or what will happen to you in the future.

But do these people *really* have psychic powers?

Actually, the amazing powers of TV psychics aren't usually any more amazing than those of stage magicians. Stage magicians don't claim to have psychic powers. They just create the *illusion* that they have them by using special tricks. I'm sure you've seen magicians make people disappear or read people's minds. Their tricks are really amazing (I can't figure out how they do it), but of course they are just *tricks*.

"I am often dishonest in my techniques, but always honest about my dishonesty . . . I happily admit cheating, as it's all part of the game."

Derren Brown (born 1971)
British TV magician

HOW CAN YOU FAKE PSYCHIC POWERS?

One of the simplest tricks magicians use to fake psychic powers is called *cold reading*. Here's a simple example:

Psychic: "I am getting someone named John . . ."
Mary: "Err . . ."
Psychic: ". . . or is it Jim?"
Mary: "Yes, I had an Uncle Jim!"
Psychic: "Correct. Your dead Uncle Jim. He says hello."
Mary: "Wow! That's amazing!"

Mary might *think* the psychic knew she had a dead uncle named Jim who is now saying hello to her. But look carefully—all the psychic did was mention two common names. When Mary didn't know anyone with the first name, the psychic tried another. The psychic didn't say whether the person was dead or alive, or even a relative. It was *Mary* who gave the psychic that information. But the psychic cleverly made it *seem* as if *he* knew those things!

3

THE GOOD, THE BAD, AND THE UGLY

"Hey, that's wrong!" we say when Tom steals Lily's bike. But what do we *mean* when we say something is wrong? And how do we know what is wrong? And what is *right*? If someone said it's *not* wrong to steal things, how could we show them they're mistaken?

These are some of the many tricky questions we'll try to answer in this chapter.

WHAT MAKES STEALING WRONG?

"Telling the truth is *right*," we say. "And stealing is *wrong*." These are things that, generally speaking, we *should*, or *should not*, do.

But *why* should we tell the truth? *Why* shouldn't we steal? What do you think makes telling the truth right and lying wrong?

Some people believe it's the results, or *consequences*, of what we do that matter.

Tom has stolen Lily's bike. By stealing the bike, Tom made himself feel happier. But he made Lily very unhappy indeed. And he made all of Lily's friends worry that their bikes will be stolen as well. So they are unhappy, too.

So, because Tom stole Lily's bike, there is *less happiness overall*. That, according to some people, is why Tom was wrong to steal the bike. We ought to do what makes people happier. We shouldn't do what makes them less happy.

HOW IMPORTANT IS HAPPINESS?

Of course, happiness is *very* important, generally speaking. But is happiness *all* that matters when it comes to right and wrong?

What about this case: Sarah's class is in big trouble. Someone has drawn a picture of the teacher on the blackboard. The picture shows the teacher with donkey's ears and a pig's tail (that's why Sarah's class is in trouble).

The teacher says she will give the *whole class* a week's detention if they don't tell her who did it. If they do tell her, she will give the naughty artist a week's detention, but no one else will suffer.

Sarah didn't draw the picture. She was in the library with the teacher—so she can't save the rest of the class by pretending she did it. But she could lie and tell the teacher that Sally drew the picture. That way, Sally will get detention, but the rest of the class won't. So, should Sarah lie and say Sally did it?

Surely it would be wrong for Sarah to blame Sally for something she didn't do, even if that makes the class a happier place overall.

So it seems that happiness isn't the only thing that matters, morally speaking.

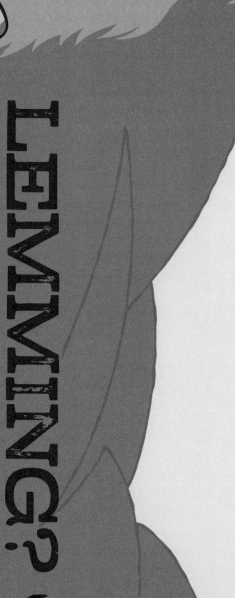

SHOULD I BE LIKE A LEMMING?

Lemmings, so the old stories go, like to copy each other. If one of them jumps off a cliff, all of them will jump off a cliff.

Should you be like a lemming? Is the right thing just to do what everyone else does? That would certainly make it easy to decide what's right and wrong. If you wanted to know whether you should steal from the supermarket, you could just look at what everyone else was doing and do the same thing.

But of course, what everyone else does isn't always the right thing, is it? Sometimes people behave in cruel and despicable ways toward other people, treating them as slaves or even killing them. If you found yourself among such people, should you do the same thing? Certainly not!

Remember, you're not a lemming. You need to make your own decisions about what is right and what is wrong.

HOW CAN I TELL RIGHT FROM WRONG?

Perhaps, if we want to know right from wrong, we should do what someone else tells us to do?

Not always. Of course, it is very often a good idea to do what others tell you—especially your parents. But there may be times in your life when people in charge will tell you to do something you shouldn't.

Here's a very famous example: in 1955, Black people in the United States were often treated very differently from white people. Many white people considered Black people inferior. Black people were even expected to give up their seats to white people on buses.

On December 1, 1955, in Alabama, a bus driver ordered a Black woman, Rosa Parks, to give up her seat to a white passenger. Rosa refused. Her refusal began a huge wave of protest about the way Black people were being treated, and led, eventually, to Black people being given equal rights.

Should Rosa Parks have given up her seat to a white person because someone in charge told her to? Of course not!

So, doing the right thing isn't just a matter of doing what everyone else does or doing what certain people tell you to do. If it were, life would be easier—you wouldn't have to think about what's right and wrong. You could just do what you were told or what everyone else did.

But unfortunately, deciding what's right and what's wrong is not as easy as that. You *do* have to think for yourself.

"People always say that I didn't give up my seat because I was tired, but that isn't true . . . No, the only tired I was, was tired of giving in."

Rosa Parks (1913–2005)
African-American civil rights activist

IS IT OKAY TO

Lots of people love animals. Many of us have pets—cats, dogs, rabbits, and guinea pigs. We are very careful to look after them and make sure they don't get sick or run over.

But why do we care about animals? Why *should* we care about them? Perhaps because, like us, animals can feel happy or sad and can suffer. My cat, Molly, can feel pain—she shrieks when I accidentally step on her tail. Molly also feels pretty happy when I feed her and very grumpy when I forget.

If animals can suffer and feel happy or sad, then surely we can't just do what we like to them? We have to take their pain and their happiness or sadness into account when deciding how to treat them.

But while we think we should take care of animals, most of us also think that it's okay to kill and eat them. In fact, we humans raise, kill, and eat billions of animals every year. The main reason we eat them is that they taste good.

But not everyone agrees that this is okay. In fact, some people think it's wrong. Many of them are vegetarians—they don't eat meat. Some are vegans—they don't eat eggs, cheese, or milk, or use any animal products at all.

How can we decide who is right about eating animals? We all agree it's wrong to kill and eat humans. But many of us think it's okay to eat other animals. And if it is okay, what's the *difference* between humans and other animals that makes it okay? Can you think of such a difference?

WILL MONEY MAKE

ME HAPPY?

Some people think that if they were rich, they would be happy. For if they had lots of money, they would never have to work again. They could spend every day doing things they really liked doing.

But does having lots of money make people happier? It turns out that, although people who win a fortune are happier *for a while*, their happiness often doesn't last long. They can afford to buy a beautiful home, an expensive car, and endless vacations. But they quickly get used to having these new things. The excitement of having new stuff wears off, and they end up feeling no happier than they were before.

We all need *some* money so we can afford the basics— food, a home, and perhaps an occasional vacation. We *think* winning a fortune will make us happier. But the truth is, while we might be happier for a while, that happiness won't last long.

What sorts of things *do* make people *truly* happy *for a long time*, do you think?

ARE WE ALL SELFISH?

Some people think that, deep down, everyone is *selfish*. They say, "The only reason anyone does anything is to make themselves feel better."

Of course, people do help others. Suppose Mary gives money to an orphanage so it can buy the children Christmas presents. Doesn't she do that because she cares about the children's happiness?

Not according to those who think everyone is selfish. They say Mary gives the money only to make *herself* feel better—so that she, and others, can think of herself as a generous and kind person. "See?" they say. "She's *still* being selfish—she's still just thinking about *herself!*"

Is it true that we care only about our own happiness?

No. Suppose an amazing pill is invented that can make you think you've given lots of money to charity. Suppose we ask Mary whether she would prefer to take the pill or really give her money to the orphans. What would she do?

If she really cared only about her own happiness, she would take the pill. That way, she could keep her money *and* feel good about thinking she'd given to the orphans. But of course Mary wouldn't choose the pill. And neither would you, I guess.

True, making other people happy can make us feel happier, too. But that's not usually the reason we do it. It seems we aren't as selfish as some people think.

IS IT WRONG TO DESIGN A BABY?

Scientists may soon reach the stage where they can design new human beings. By making changes to the first cell from which a new life begins, scientists can change what sort of human being it grows into.

Scientists can't change very much now, but it may not be long until you will be able to choose what color eyes and hair your child has, how intelligent, and perhaps even how beautiful he or she is. Perhaps scientists will be able to eliminate ugliness!

But should we allow parents to do this? Should people be allowed to design their own baby?

Some people say, "No! A human being is not just a thing, like a handbag or a coat! There's nothing wrong with designer bags and coats, but designer babies are a different matter! Humans are far too important to be treated as fashion items. No one should be allowed to design a baby."

Do you agree? It's certainly true that it's wrong to treat another human being as nothing more than an extension of our wardrobe. Someone who chose to have a blue-eyed baby just to match their favorite coat would be a very selfish and shallow person.

But what if you wanted to design your baby to help the *baby*, not yourself?

We don't think it is wrong that parents help their children grow up to be as smart and as beautiful as possible by sending them to good schools and to dentists who can straighten their teeth.

But if it's okay to help children grow up to be smart and beautiful using schools and dentists *after they are born*, what's wrong with using science to design them that way *in the first place*? Is it wrong? People strongly disagree!

BRAIN BURN!
Do stories such as Frankenstein suggest it's wrong to interfere with nature?

SEEING AND BELIEVING

Most of the questions in this chapter are about knowledge.

People claim to know a great many things, of course.
I'm sure I know Paris is the capital city of France. Other
people claim to know that astrology works, that they've
been abducted by aliens, and that miracles happen. Some
even claim to know that fairies exist.

But what *is* knowledge? And how can we tell when we've
really got it?

WHAT IS KNOWLEDGE?

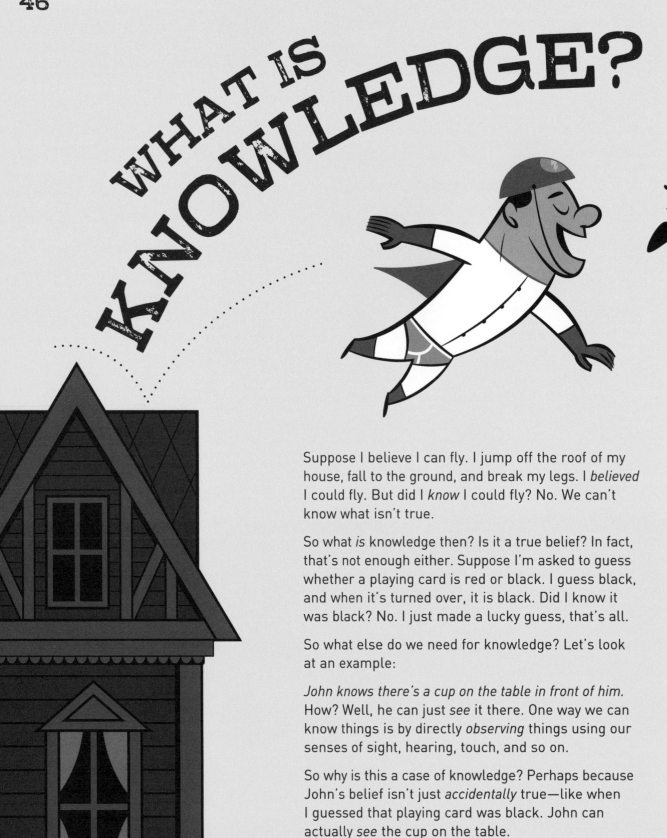

Suppose I believe I can fly. I jump off the roof of my house, fall to the ground, and break my legs. I *believed* I could fly. But did I *know* I could fly? No. We can't know what isn't true.

So what *is* knowledge then? Is it a true belief? In fact, that's not enough either. Suppose I'm asked to guess whether a playing card is red or black. I guess black, and when it's turned over, it is black. Did I know it was black? No. I just made a lucky guess, that's all.

So what else do we need for knowledge? Let's look at an example:

John knows there's a cup on the table in front of him. How? Well, he can just *see* it there. One way we can know things is by directly *observing* things using our senses of sight, hearing, touch, and so on.

So why is this a case of knowledge? Perhaps because John's belief isn't just *accidentally* true—like when I guessed that playing card was black. John can actually *see* the cup on the table.

Observation is one important way of gaining knowledge.

WHY IS IT IMPORTANT TO KNOW STUFF?

If you just believe whatever you want and don't worry about knowing anything, you'll soon end up in big, big trouble.

If you believe that you can fly just by flapping your arms, you're going to have a short life!

CAN I MAKE SOMETHING TRUE BY BELIEVING IT?

Sometimes. Suppose I have to jump across a river. If I doubt I'll make it, it's more likely I'll fail. Being confident can help me succeed. Really believing I'll succeed can help my belief come true.

But of course, this is a special case. You can't usually make something true by believing it. Not even if we all believe it. If we all believed we could fly and all jumped off a cliff together, we'd still all plummet to the ground.

Ouch.

WHEN SHOULD WE BE LIKE SHERLOCK HOLMES?

Sometimes we can just *see* that something is true. I can just see that there's a book in front of me now, for example.

But how do we know about things we *can't* observe? That's when we need to act like the great detective Sherlock Holmes and look for *evidence*.

We can't look back in time, into Earth's distant past. No one has ever seen a living dinosaur. But we know dinosaurs walked the earth long ago because we have evidence—fossils buried in the ground and huge footprints pressed into ancient rock.

And we can't see into the future either. We can't experience tomorrow before tomorrow arrives.

Take this chair I'm about to sit on. How do I know it will support me? I have to rely on evidence. I believe the chair will support me because it has always done so up to now.

DOES HAVING GOOD EVIDENCE MEAN WE CAN'T BE WRONG?

No. Just because we have really good evidence that something is true doesn't mean we can't be *wrong*.

Remember that chair I was about to sit on? I believe that it will support me when I sit on it, and I have excellent *evidence* for this—the chair looks strong, and it's never collapsed before.

Of course, it's still *possible* the chair will collapse. Maybe it's been eaten away by termites. But that's very unlikely, given the evidence. I am still justified in believing the chair will hold my weight.

So just because it's *possible* we're mistaken about something doesn't mean that we don't have good evidence that it's true, or that we aren't justified in believing that it's true.

CAN SCIENTISTS PROVE DINOSAURS WALKED THE EARTH?

Sometimes people say, "Scientists can't prove anything! They can't prove anything they haven't actually observed. So they can't prove dinosaurs walked the earth!"

But is this true? Yes, it's always possible scientists have gotten something wrong. But of course, that doesn't mean they don't have excellent evidence—good enough that they're justified in feeling sure.

After all, in court people are sent to prison for committing crimes no one else saw them commit. But if the evidence is strong enough, the judge and jury are still justified in sending the person to jail. We say the person is proved guilty *beyond reasonable doubt*.

Scientists can also prove things beyond reasonable doubt. They can prove beyond reasonable doubt that dinosaurs walked the earth.

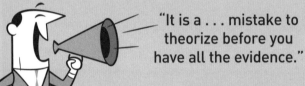

"It is a . . . mistake to theorize before you have all the evidence."

Sherlock Holmes
From *A Study in Scarlet* (1888)
by Sir Arthur Conan Doyle

CAN I ALWAYS BELIEVE MY EYES?

Most of the time, our eyes are pretty reliable. We can, just by looking, find out what's in front of us. And our other senses (smell, hearing, taste, and touch) are pretty reliable when it comes to detecting smells, sounds, and so on.

But of course, sometimes our senses can mislead us. Sometimes what we experience is an *illusion*, when how things *seem* is not how they *really* are. Take a look at these two lines:

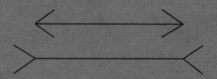

Which line is longer? The top one looks shorter, doesn't it? But if you use a ruler to measure the lines, you will discover they are exactly the same length.

Now look at this picture. Does it look like it's moving? It isn't, of course. Focus on just one of the blobs and the picture should stop moving for a few seconds.

These illusions show that our senses can't always be trusted. So, when they reveal something very peculiar, or when it's particularly important we get something right, it's worth thinking about whether our senses might be tricking us.

The Devil's Fork is a common optical illusion.

ARE THERE SUCH THINGS AS
FLYING SAUCERS?

Back in 1947, pilot Kenneth Arnold was flying his small plane near Mount Rainier in Washington State. Suddenly he noticed something peculiar in the sky—a series of strange objects moving in a line. When he landed, Arnold reported the objects, and soon radio stations and newspapers were reporting what Arnold saw—a line of flying saucers!

Soon afterward, other people reported seeing saucer-shaped objects in the sky. And, of course, we've been seeing them ever since.

You might think that because so many people have reported flying saucers, at least *some* real flying saucers must have visited Earth.

But here's an interesting fact. Actually, Arnold *didn't* see saucers. He said the objects *moved* like saucers skipping across a lake as they gently bounced along. But they looked like *boomerangs*. Unfortunately, the reporter who noted down Arnold's story got it wrong.

So why is it that, straight after the news reports of "flying saucers," thousands of other people saw saucers too? Many of them probably saw *something*—a light in the sky maybe—and because they *expected* it to be saucer-shaped, that's how it looked to them. Their eyes deceived them.

This effect is called the *power of suggestion*. Arnold's story is just one of countless examples of its extraordinary ability to fool people. Have you ever been fooled by the power of suggestion?

Do you notice anything strange
about this dog's legs?

DOES ASTROLOGY REALLY WORK?

I am sure you've seen astrology columns in magazines and newspapers that predict what will happen to you that week. For example:

Sagittarius: This week brings good news and bad. While a friend will have some luck, money may be a worry for you. Toward the end of the week, things will start to look up.

How are astrologers able to make their predictions? They believe the positions of the stars and planets have an influence on your life. They make astrology charts showing where the stars and planets are moving, and they base their predictions on these charts.

But can astrologers really predict what will happen just by looking at someone's star chart?

Actually, what astrologers predict does often seem to come true! Is that good evidence that astrology really works?

Maybe not.

Notice that astrologers often predict what's quite likely to be true anyway. They say things like:

You will think about changing your job.
You will worry about money.

Most grownups think about changing their job and worry about money. So the fact that such predictions often come true isn't good evidence that astrology works.

Also, what astrologers predict is often very vague. Take the prediction *"Things will start to look up."* What does this *mean*? Does it mean *I* will have some luck? Or that things will improve for the *country as a whole*? Or something *else*? Whatever happens—even if I happen to be run over by a bus—it's not hard to find a sense in which *things start to look up*.

And remember that if, like astrologers, you make enough predictions, you are bound to get some right just by chance!

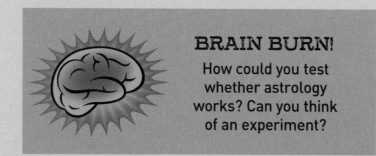

BRAIN BURN!

How could you test whether astrology works? Can you think of an experiment?

DOES BLEEDING
PEOPLE MAKE THEM
BETTER?

A few hundred years ago, a popular treatment for sick people was bleeding. Doctors would cut open sick people's veins to let out the "bad blood."

Why did doctors do this? Well, they noticed that people who were bled often got better. So they supposed that it was the bleeding that had made them better.

We now know that bleeding doesn't make people better. It can make them even more sick. The fact that many people get better after being bled is not good evidence that bleeding works—because lots of people will get better anyway, even if they aren't bled!

IS TIME TRAVEL

There are lots of stories and films about time travel. But could someone *really* travel through time? And if they could, what would it be like?

In H. G. Wells's story *The Time Machine*, the time traveler climbs onboard his homemade machine, dials in a year in the distant future, and pulls a lever.

Time starts to pass more quickly around him. Someone walks across the room at the speed of a rocket, and the Sun shoots rapidly across the sky. Soon the years are flying by in the blink of an eye until finally the traveler comes to a stop in the distant future.

But does this make sense?

Surely, if the time traveler is in the room and able to see people flitting in and out like flies, then they must also be able to see him! Although if they seem to him to be moving about very quickly, he must seem to them to be moving very slowly or not at all. He'll seem frozen like a statue!

How does that help him travel through time?

Hasn't he just slowed himself down? Does this really count as *time travel*?

POSSIBLE?

Some scientists think that time travel *is* possible. There might be strange *wormholes* in space that allow shortcuts through time. But even if the scientists could prove time travel is possible, there are still some *philosophical problems* that need to be solved.

One problem is about the *past*. If you really had a time machine and could go back to visit the past, then you could go back and *change what has already happened*.

But if you could go back and change the past, then you could go back and murder your grandfather before he has any children.

That would prevent yourself from ever being born!

But hang on—if you aren't born, then *you won't exist*. And you won't be able to go back in time to murder your poor old grandfather and change the past. So you *will* still be born! So you both will exist and won't exist! Impossible!

Some people think that the impossibility of going back and preventing yourself from being born shows that time travel must be impossible. But I'm not so sure . . .

DO ALIENS ABDUCT PEOPLE?

Hundreds of people every year claim they have been *abducted by aliens.* Often the kidnappers from outer space are supposed to give their victims strange medical examinations. The abductions usually happen at night—the victims wake up and find themselves being taken away.

Despite the hundreds of reports, there is *no other evidence* that anyone has ever been abducted by aliens. There's just *what people say* has happened to them.

So how likely is it that people are being whisked away by aliens?

Perhaps part of the explanation for these claims lies in a strange, dreamlike state called *sleep paralysis.* During sleep paralysis, you think you have woken up, but you haven't. Your body seems paralyzed, and often bizarre things appear to happen. Sometimes you see strange beings that look like demons or aliens.

Of course, the creatures people experience during sleep paralysis aren't actually there. But they can seem frighteningly real.

Sleep paralysis probably does explain some of the alien-abduction stories.

ARE THERE REALLY MIRACLES?

Every year, people report miracles. Some are religious miracles. The Catholic Church claims there have been many cases where people have prayed to a Catholic saint for someone's disease to be cured, and the disease has miraculously vanished.

But do miracles *really* happen? In a way, they do. That's because when we say a miracle happened, we just mean there has been an amazing, fortunate coincidence.

Suppose I am almost broke. I can't pay my bills. I get so desperate that I buy a lottery ticket. And I win! All my money problems are solved! That would be a kind of miracle, wouldn't it? And such miracles do happen.

In fact, what would really be amazing is if such miracles *didn't* happen. A lottery winner is amazingly lucky. But of course, *someone* has to win, so someone is bound to be amazingly lucky. That some people are amazingly lucky is no more surprising than that some people are amazingly *unlucky,* such as people struck by lightning.

Whether saints, gods, or other supernatural beings ever perform miracles by changing what's going on in our lives—well, that's another question entirely!

DO FAIRIES EXIST?

In 1917, two little girls, Elsie and Frances, lived in a small village called Cottingley in northern England. One day, they took their little Kodak Brownie camera out to the woods—and photographed themselves playing with fairies!

Their photos became famous and impressed, among others, the author Sir Arthur Conan Doyle, who wrote the Sherlock Holmes detective stories. Conan Doyle was quite convinced the Cottingley fairies were real.

Even photographic experts said they could not see how the images had been faked. They said one of the fairies seemed to be blurred, as if it had been moving when the photo was taken.

In 1982, 65 years later, the two girls—now elderly women—finally admitted their fairies were paper cut-outs that they had drawn themselves.

The Cottingley fairies had inspired a whole generation to believe in fairies—but those fairies, at least, weren't real.

"Miracles happen every day—change your perception of what a miracle is and you'll see them all around you."

Jon Bon Jovi (born 1962)
American rock singer

GLOSSARY

Words in **bold** refer to other glossary entries.

ABDUCT To kidnap someone—to take them away using force.

ANCESTOR Someone from whom you are descended. Your parents, grandparents, great-grandparents, and so on are your ancestors.

ASTROLOGY Astrology is based on the idea that the movements of stars and planets have a (probably **supernatural**) influence on our lives. Astrologers predict what will happen to people based on where the stars and planets are.

ATOMS Incredibly small particles from which all **physical** objects are made.

BELIEVE If you believe something, you think it is **true**. I believe that Earth goes around the Sun. Not all beliefs are true, of course.

BIG BANG A huge explosion that created the universe, including time and space. The big bang took place about 13 billion years ago.

BRAIN The big, walnut-shaped, gray-colored organ inside your skull.

COLD READING One of the tricks that people who are pretending to be **psychic** use to convince others that they have amazing, **supernatural** powers.

DARWIN, CHARLES Darwin (1809–1882) was one of the greatest **scientists** ever to have lived. He developed the theory of **natural selection**, which explains how new **species** can evolve gradually over long periods of time.

DEMOCRITUS An ancient Greek **philosopher** (c. 460–370 B.C.) who believed that **physical** objects are made from **atoms**.

ELEMENTS The elements are the basic kinds of stuff from which everything is made. **Empedocles** believed there were four elements: earth, air, fire, and water.

EMPEDOCLES An ancient Greek **philosopher** (c. 490–430 B.C.) who believed that the universe is made up of four **elements**.

EVIDENCE Facts that support a **theory**—that make the theory more likely to be **true**. The fact that every cat I have ever seen has ears supports the theory that all cats have ears.

EVOLUTION The gradual process by which **species** of plants, animals, or other living things change, sometimes producing a whole new species. Charles **Darwin**'s theory of **natural selection** explains one of the main ways in which species evolve.

EXPERIENCE We experience the world around us using our **senses**—these include taste, touch, smell, hearing, and sight.

HERACLITUS The ancient Greek **philosopher** (c. 535–475 B.C.) who is supposed to have believed that you cannot jump into the same river twice.

HUMAN A **species** of two-legged **primate** that appeared about 200,000 years ago.

ILLUSION An experience that is misleading. Mirages are one famous type of illusion in which people seem to see things in hot deserts that are not really there.

JUSTIFIED One way in which you can be justified in **believing** something is if you have good **evidence** that it is **true**.

KNOWLEDGE Although knowledge is something we all want, it's tricky to define exactly what it is. See pages 46–47 for some ideas.

MEDIUM A medium is someone who claims that they can communicate with the dead.

MIRACLE An amazing and wonderful event—perhaps a **supernatural** event.

MORAL Moral means "having to do with morality." A morality is a system of rules about right and **wrong**—about what we should or should not do.

NATURAL SELECTION A theory developed by Charles **Darwin** that explains one of the main ways in which **species** evolve.

NEURONS Tiny cells that transmit electrical impulses around your **brain** and body.

OBSERVE We observe the world around us using our **senses**—these include taste, touch, smell, hearing, and sight.

PARKS, ROSA The African-American woman who, in 1955, refused to give up her seat on a bus to a white person (as Black people were expected to do at that time). Rosa Parks's action began a huge movement for equal rights for Black people.

PHILOSOPHER A philosopher tries to answer some of the biggest questions of all, such as "Why does the universe exist?" and "What makes things right and **wrong**?"

PHYSICAL Physical objects, such as ants, chairs, and planets, are located in space (my table is in my bedroom, for example) and have physical dimensions, such as height, width, and weight.

POWER OF SUGGESTION When people are affected by the power of suggestion, they are likely to see what they expect to see—even when it's not there!

PREDICTION **Theories** let us make predictions. The theory that all cats have ears allows me to predict that the next cat I see will have ears.

PRIMATE A member of a family of about 230 different mammal **species** that includes lemurs, monkeys, apes, and modern **humans**.

PSYCHIC Someone who has a **miraculous**, **supernatural** ability to **experience** or know things hidden from the rest of us. People who claim to be psychic often say they can communicate with the dead or can actually "see" things happening in the future. There is no good scientific **evidence** that anyone really does have such amazing powers.

RELIGION A religion is a set of beliefs about the **supernatural**. Religions often tell a story about the creation of the world and living things. Most religions involve worshiping a god or gods.

ROBOT An intelligent machine that can be programmed to carry out tasks.

SCIENTIST Someone who uses **observation** to find **evidence** to both support and test their **theories** about how the world works.

SENSE Our five main senses are taste, touch, hearing, sight, and smell. Our senses allow us to **observe** the world around us.

SLEEP PARALYSIS A strange state in which you are still asleep but think you are awake. You are unable to move, and sometimes strange creatures seem to appear.

SPECIES A group of similar living things that can breed together and produce offspring. **Humans** are a species; chimpanzees are another. There are also different species of plants, fish, flowers, and so on.

SUPERNATURAL Nature prevents human beings from jumping 30 feet in the air or coming back from the dead. A supernatural being—such as a vampire, an angel, or a god—may do things that nature otherwise prevents. They may also exist outside of the natural world (heaven, for example, is often thought of as a supernatural place—a place that's not part of the natural world). Some people, such as **psychics**, claim they have supernatural powers and can communicate with supernatural beings (including the dead).

THEORY A theory is a claim about the world that goes beyond what we have actually **observed** to be **true**. That my cat has ears is not a theory: I can see she has ears. That all cats, including the ones not even born yet, have ears, is a theory.

TRUE A claim is true if it says how things really are (rather than, say, just how we **believe** them to be).

WRONG Something is **morally** wrong if it is something we should not do—something we could be blamed for doing.

INDEX

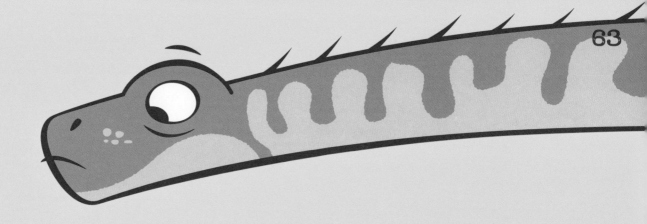

FURTHER READING

Books

The Philosophy Files by Stephen Law
The Philosophy Files 2 by Stephen Law
The Philosophy Gym by Stephen Law
The Magic Detectives by Joe Nickell
Philosophy for Kids: 40 Fun Questions That Help You Wonder . . . about Everything! by David A. White
100 Science Experiments by Georgina Andrews and Kate Knighton

Websites

Illusions:
https://kids.niehs.nih.gov/games/riddles/illusions/index.htm

Weird stuff:
www.skeptic.com/junior_skeptic

NASA kids' club:
www.nasa.gov/kidsclub/index.html

Thinking tips

Here are five tips to help you think about big questions. When you are trying to answer a big question:

1. Try to construct an argument to show you have the right answer—that means coming up with good reasons for why your answer must be the correct one.

2. Get creative. Don't be scared to try something really different!

3. Try to test your answer by thinking of how someone would argue against you.

4. Try to be as clear and straightforward as you can. Don't make your answer more complicated than it needs to be!

5. Don't be scared to question what other people take for granted. Sometimes the solution to a puzzle lies in questioning what others have just assumed is true.